Our thanks to Cleve Jones for his life, his work, his inspiration, and for his kind assistance with this project.

In memory of Ron—first high school friend, first friend lost to AIDS—*RS*

For Justin, Mac, Bobby, Jeff, and John, my dear Cleveland crew—always there for me through the years and the best company on the dance floor—*JC*

Magination Press
Books for Kids From the
American Psychological Association

Text copyright © 2021 by Rob Sanders. Illustrations copyright © 2021 by Jamey Christoph. Published in 2021 by Magination Press, an imprint of the American Psychological Association. All rights reserved. Except as permitted under the United States Copyright Act of 1976, no part of this publication may be reproduced or distributed in any form or by any means, or stored in a database or retrieval system, without the prior written permission of the publisher.

Magination Press is a registered trademark of the American Psychological Association. Order books at maginationpress.org, or call 1-800-374-2721.

Book design by Rachel Ross
Printed by Phoenix Color, Hagerstown, MD

Library of Congress Cataloging-in-Publication Data
Names: Sanders, Rob, 1958- author. | Christoph, Jamey, 1980- illustrator.
Title: Stitch by stitch: Cleve Jones and the AIDS memorial Quilt/by Rob Sanders; illustrated by Jamey Christoph.
Description: Washington, DC : Magination Press, [2021] | "American Psychological Association." | Summary: Determined not to let history forget those who died of AIDS, activist Cleve Jones creates a memorial quilt to commemorate the lives of those lost and bring awareness to the disease. Includes a timeline and other backmatter. Identifiers: LCCN 2020055701 (print) | LCCN 2020055702 (ebook) | ISBN 9781433837395 (hardcover) | ISBN 9781433837401 (ebook)
Subjects: LCSH: Jones, Cleve—Juvenile fiction. | CYAC: Jones, Cleve—Fiction. | NAMES Project AIDS Memorial Quilt—Fiction. | AIDS (Disease)—Fiction.
Classification: LCC PZ7.S19785 St 2021 (print) | LCC PZ7.S19785 (ebook) | DDC [E]—dc23
LC record available at https://lccn.loc.gov/2020055701
LC ebook record available at https://lccn.loc.gov/2020055702

Manufactured in the United States of America
10 9 8 7 6 5 4 3 2 1

Stitch by Stitch

Cleve Jones and the
AIDS Memorial Quilt

by Rob Sanders   illustrated by Jamey Christoph

Magination Press · Washington, DC · American Psychological Association

Piece by piece.

Stitch by stitch.

That's how a quilt is made.

Before Cleve Jones was born, his great-grandmother sewed a quilt for him.

Cutting and pinning together fabric scraps.

Stitching the pieces together.

The quilt welcomed Cleve home as a newborn on October 11, 1954.

Cleve napped with the quilt,

and felt it tuck around him when he was sick.

The quilt warmed him, like the love that stitched it together.

As Cleve grew older, life wasn't easy for him.

Even the warmth of a quilt couldn't help when he was bullied.

Then things went from bad to worse.

Pictures
1971

When he was 18, Cleve told his parents he was gay.

They didn't approve.

As soon as he could, Cleve left home.

He'd heard of a place where there *might* be others like him.

A place where he *might* fit in.

San Francisco, California.

One by one.

Person by person.

That's how friendships are made.

Cleve soon had a patchwork of friends.

They were alike and different.

The friends were held together by a common thread.

They were people on the fringes.

On the outside.

Often without family.

Searching for acceptance.

Action by action.

Voice by voice.

That's how a movement is made.

Cleve worked for Harvey Milk.

Harvey was an openly gay politician.

A leader in San Francisco.

A mentor for Cleve.

Cleve was there when Harvey was elected to office in 1977.

Members of the LGBTQ+ community were being treated unfairly.

They weren't given the same rights as others.

Harvey, Cleve, and others in the community decided something had to be done.

Cleve went to college and started working for equal rights.

Little by little, things were changing.

Then came the day when Harvey Milk and Mayor George Moscone were assassinated.

Cleve and his friends were angry. Sad. Hurt.

Their feelings came rumbling out on the streets.

Anger and hatred towards the community began to grow.

Progress unraveled right before their eyes.

Then things went from bad to worse.

Healthy young gay men began to be diagnosed with unusual symptoms.

Their illnesses grew worse and worse.

Most never got better.

Many died.

Pieces of the quilt of friendship were lost. Forever.

The illness spread from one city to another.

From state to state.

From country to country.

The disease became an epidemic.

Finally, it was given a name: Acquired Immunodeficiency Syndrome, or AIDS.

Most people didn't seem to care that others were dying.

Even some doctors.

Even the United States government.

Many people looked down on those with AIDS.

Some said they deserved it.

Most thought they could never
get AIDS themselves.

But AIDS continued to spread.
To every community.

And throughout the world.

Out of the blue.

Unexpectedly.

That's how an idea begins.

On November 27, 1985, Cleve Jones led a candlelight march to remember Harvey Milk and Mayor Moscone.

Cleve and his friend, Joseph Durant, handed out cardboard and markers.

"Write down the name of someone you know who died of AIDS," Cleve called.

Some people in the crowd wrote initials.

Some wrote only a first name.

Some wrote nothing.

Then a man took two pieces of cardboard, taped them together, and wrote his brother's full name in large letters.

Soon, others wrote the names of their friends and family members who had died because of AIDS.

One by one the names were taped to the wall of the Federal Building.

Through rain,
Cleve looked at
the names pieced
together on
the wall.

Suddenly, he had an idea.
He would create a symbol.
A memorial.
A quilt.

It took a year and a half for the idea to become a reality.

With spray paint and fabric, Cleve and Joseph created the first two Quilt panels.

Others made panels, too.

Gert McMullin volunteered to sew the panels together.

That year, during the Lesbian and Gay Pride Parade, 40 panels were displayed at City Hall in San Francisco.

News of the Quilt began to spread.

Family members and friends began to cut and pin together fabric scraps.

They stitched the pieces together, creating three-foot-by-six-foot Quilt panels.

It was a way to remember,

a way to heal,

a way to show love,

a way to do something when it seemed nothing could be done.

Slowly.

Over time.

One step at a time.

That's how change is made.

On October 11, 1987—Cleve's birthday—squares of stitched-together panels were unfolded and placed on the lawn of the National Mall in Washington, DC.

The ground was quilted with names.

Each was read aloud.

The AIDS Memorial Quilt toured towns and cities. Then things changed again.

People began to discuss AIDS.

People with AIDS began to receive help.

Money poured in for research.

Doctors began to find treatments.

The government began taking action.

Memory by memory.

Panel by panel.

That's how a memorial was made.

Today the panels on the Quilt represent 100,000 names,

100,000 individuals,

100,000 people who will be remembered forever.

Cleve called it "a monument sewn of fabric and thread."

Piece by piece.   One by one.

Action by action.   Out of the blue.

Over time.   Memory by memory.

Cleve Jones still has the quilt his great-grandmother made.

The quilt he napped with, and that tucked around him when he was sick.

It warms him to this day, like the love that stitched it together.

Cleve's first quilt inspired another— one with names.

A Quilt that remembers.

A Quilt that made a difference.

That's how a monument was sewn of fabric and thread.

Discussion Guide

When reading any book of nonfiction, questions may arise. It is also to be expected that children's questions may go deeper and deeper with each reading of a book. Create an atmosphere where children feel their questions are welcome by being honest, succinct, and by providing answers based in fact. Feel free to ask a child, "What do you think?" or "What are you feeling?" Remember, you don't have to have an answer to every question. There's nothing wrong with saying, "I don't know," or "Let me think about that." The following are some sample responses to questions that children may have after reading *Stitch by Stitch*.

Q: Is there a cure for AIDS today?

A: Since the 1980s, thanks to medical advances, medication has helped people living with HIV lead full lives. However, people who aren't treated can still die of complications caused by AIDS.

Q: How do people get HIV/AIDS?

A: HIV/AIDS is difficult to get. It is not like a cold or the flu. HIV/AIDS can be passed from person to person through unprotected sex, sharing needles, and in other ways. The most important things to know are that the transmission of HIV/AIDS can be prevented, that there are treatments if someone is diagnosed with HIV/AIDS, and that you can be friends with someone who has HIV/AIDS without worry.

Q: Was HIV/AIDS just a disease that gay men got?

A: It may have seemed that way at first, but over time doctors and scientists realized that anyone could contract the disease. Those doctors and scientists also discovered that the disease could be prevented and treated.

Q: Why didn't the government do anything about AIDS?

A: At the time, people who got HIV/AIDS were seen as people living on the fringes of society, like Cleve and his friends. Members of the LGBTQ+ community were already being discriminated against and treated unfairly. Ignoring their illness was another form of discrimination.

Q: What is discrimination and why does it happen?

A: Discrimination is the unfair treatment of people or groups of people based on who they are. People are discriminated against because of race, gender, age, sexual orientation, and other characteristics. Discrimination often is caused by fear, misunderstanding, anger, and/or hate.

Glossary

AIDS—Acquired Immunodeficiency Syndrome; a disease that attacks the immune system

assassinated—killed for political or religious reasons

epidemic—a widespread occurrence of an infectious disease

gay—used to describe a person who loves and is attracted to a person of the same gender, often used to describe men in the LGBTQ+ community

HIV—Human Immunodeficiency Virus; a virus that interferes with the body's ability to fight infections and can lead to AIDS

lesbian—a woman who loves and is attracted to other women

LGBTQ+—Lesbian, gay, bisexual, transgender, queer, or questioning. The + represents all the other identities of those in the community. When the events of this story occurred, the community was often referred to only as the gay community or the lesbian and gay community. However, those terms left out many vital members of the larger community.

on the fringes—outside of, different from, or not favored by the majority

quilt—a padded bed covering enclosed by fabric stitched in place

Cleve Jones

Cleve Jones was born on October 11, 1954 in West Lafayette, Indiana. His family moved to Scottsdale, Arizona when he was 14. After high school, Cleve attended Arizona State University. Along with his mother, Cleve was a Quaker. What he learned as a Quaker later influenced his nonviolent approach to demonstrations and civil disobedience. He came out about being gay when he turned 18. His parents did not approve. Shortly after, he moved to San Francisco, California.

Cleve quickly made friends in San Francisco and found others who were like him. He had a number of odd jobs after first moving to the city, and soon met gay-rights leader Harvey Milk. Cleve worked as a student intern in Milk's office while studying political science at San Francisco State University. Harvey and San Francisco's Mayor George Moscone were assassinated on November 27, 1978.

Cleve Jones continued his gay activism, and worked for a time in the district office of State Assemblyman Art Agnos. In 1983, when the AIDS crisis was beginning, Cleve co-founded the San Francisco AIDS Foundation. He had the idea for what would become the NAME Project AIDS Memorial Quilt during a candlelight memorial for Harvey Milk in 1985. Cleve created the first panel for the quilt in 1987 in honor of his friend Marvin Feldman.

Cleve Jones' activism continued as he championed causes from gay rights to HIV/AIDS to marriage equality. In recent years, he has worked with UNITE HERE, a labor union of hospitality workers with a diverse membership that seeks to achieve greater equality and opportunity for its members.

Diagnosed with AIDS in the 1980s, Cleve responded well to early trials of a drug "cocktail" that fought the virus. He lives in San Francisco, California.

Meet Gert McMullin

"THE MOTHER OF THE QUILT"

When Cleve Jones called the first meeting to gather volunteers to work on the Quilt, only two people showed up. One of them was Cindi "Gert" McMullin. Initially, Gert created two Quilt panels, but she quickly became an integral part of the larger Quilt project. She was there in 1987 when the Quilt was first displayed on the National Mall in Washington, DC, she traveled to Europe for Quilt displays, and she rang Tibetan bells as the names of those memorialized on the Quilt were called—and through it all, she sewed. Gert made Quilt panels, repaired damaged ones, and sewed panels together to form the larger Quilt. Gert was given the title of Head of Quilt Production, but Cleve calls her "The Mother of the Quilt" because of the dedication and care she continues to show for it. When the headquarters for the NAMES Project AIDS Memorial Quilt was moved to Atlanta, Georgia, Gert went, too. And when the Quilt returned home to San Francisco in 2019, Gert also returned. In 2020, when another pandemic plagued the world, Gert used fabric remnants from the AIDS Memorial Quilt to make face masks. The masks were distributed in the San Francisco Bay Area. Stitch by stitch, Gert McMullin continues to make a difference.

Sources

Cleve Jones & Jeff Dawson (2000). *Stitching a Revolution: The Making of an Activist*. HarperOne.

Cleve Jones (2016). *When We Rise: My Life in the Movement*. Hachette Books.

Frontline (R), WEDU, PBS (2006, May 30). *The Age of AIDS: Interview with Cleve Jones*. http://www.pbs.org/wgbhpages/frontline/aids/interviews/jones.html

For Further Reading

Jennine Atkins (1999). *A Name on the Quilt: A Story of Remembrance*. Aladdin.

AIDS MEMORIAL QUILT TIMELINE

1985

November 27—Cleve Jones has the idea for the Quilt during a march to remember Harvey Milk and Mayor George Moscone.

1987

Cleve Jones and Joseph Durant make the first two panels of the Quilt.

June—40 panels are displayed during the Lesbian and Gay Pride Parade.

Cleve, Mike Smith, Gert McMullin, and others organize the NAMES Project Foundation.

October 11—The Quilt is displayed for the first time on the National Mall in Washington, DC. The 1,920 panels cover a space larger than the size of a football field. Half a million people visit the Quilt.

1988

Spring—The Quilt is taken on a four-month, 20-city, national tour. The Quilt triples to 6,000 panels.

October—With 8,288 panels, the Quilt is displayed on the Ellipse in front of the White House.

December 1—The first World AIDS Day is held.

1989

A second tour of North America takes the Quilt to 19 cities in the United States and Canada.

October—The Quilt is again displayed on the Ellipse in Washington, DC.

1992

Panels from every state and 28 countries are now part of the AIDS Memorial Quilt.

October—The entire Quilt is displayed in Washington, DC.

Common Threads: Stories from the Quilt is released by HBO.

1993

January—The NAMES Project marches in President Bill Clinton's inaugural parade.

1996

October—The entire AIDS Memorial Quilt is displayed for the last time in Washington, DC. The Quilt covers the National Mall. President Bill Clinton and First Lady Hillary Clinton visit the Quilt. He is the first president to do so.

2000

The NAMES Project headquarters are moved to Atlanta, Georgia.

2004

June 26—The 8,000 newest panels are displayed on The Ellipse in Washington, DC.

2019

The National AIDS Memorial becomes the permanent caretaker of the Quilt.

The Quilt returns to San Francisco, California.

Information in the section above was adapted from aidsmemorial.org/quilt-history.

LEARN MORE
To learn more about the National AIDS Memorial and the Quilt, visit aidsmemorial.org.
To experience a virtual exhibition of all 48,000 panels of the AIDS Memorial Quilt, visit aidsmemorial.org/virtual-exhibition.

THE FIRST DECADE OF AIDS IN AMERICA

1981

June—Cases of a rare lung infection and a rare, aggressive cancer are first reported in New York City and Los Angeles.

By the end of 1981, there are 337 known cases of severe immune deficiency and 130 of the cases have resulted in death.

1982

September—The CDC uses the term AIDS (Acquired Immunodeficiency Syndrome) for the first time.

December—An infant, who received blood transfusions, is diagnosed with AIDS.

1983

A conference is held to determine guidelines for testing blood for HIV. No decision is reached.

Cases of AIDS in females are first reported.

The U.S. Congress approves funds for AIDS research and treatment.

The CDC states that HIV cannot be transferred through casual contact.

The first AIDS discrimination lawsuit is filed.

1984

The cause of AIDS is discovered, and a blood test is developed to diagnose AIDS.

1985

The first commercial drug test for HIV is released.

Ryan White, an Indiana teenager with AIDS, is refused entry into school.

September 17—President Ronald Reagan mentions AIDS publicly for the first time, years after the first cases were reported.

At least one HIV case is reported in every region of the world.

Cleve Jones has the idea for a memorial quilt.

1986

The first panels of the AIDS Memorial Quilt are created.

The virus causing AIDS is officially named HIV (Human Immunodeficiency Virus).

1987

The first antiretroviral drug–AZT–is approved by the U.S. Food and Drug Administration.

The AIDS Memorial Quilt is displayed in Washington, DC for the first time.

A federal judge orders the Desoto County School Board to admit the Ray brothers–Ricky, Robert, and Randy–to school. The boys are hemophiliacs who have contracted HIV. The town is outraged, and the Rays' home is set on fire.

1988

December 1 is declared World AIDS Day.

Ryan White testifies before the President's Commission on AIDS.

The Pediatric AIDS Foundation is formed.

The first national HIV/AIDS educational program is launched.

1989

Congress creates the National Commission on AIDS.

100,000 cases of AIDS are reported in the U.S.

1990

The CDC reports the transmission of AIDS through a dental procedure.

April 8—Ryan White dies of AIDS.

Congress creates the Americans with Disabilities Act. It prohibits discrimination against people with disabilities—including HIV and AIDS.

Congress creates the Ryan White Comprehensive AIDS Resources Emergency (CARE) Act. It provides 220.5 million dollars to use for community-based care and treatment in its first year.

AZT is approved for use with pediatric AIDS.

1991

The Red Ribbon Project is launched.

By the end of the year, 160,969 cases of AIDS had been reported, resulting in 120,453 deaths.

Information in the section above was adapted from aids.gov/hiv-aids-basics/hiv-aids-101/aids-timeline and amfar.org/thirty-years-of-hiv/aids-snapshots-of-an-epidemic.

Stitch by Stitch

By Rob Sanders

Author's Note

Before this book was written, I wrote the below poem about Cleve and the AIDS Memorial Quilt.
This poem is woven throughout the text of the book. Below you will find the poem in its entirety.

Piece by piece.

Stitch by stitch.

That's how a quilt is made.

One by one.

Person by person.

That's how friendships are made.

Action by action.

Voice by voice.

That's how a movement is made.

Out of the blue.

Unexpectedly.

That's how an idea begins.

Slowly.

Over time.

One step at a time.

That's how change is made.

Memory by memory.

Panel by panel.

That's how a memorial was made.

Piece by piece.

One by one.

Action by action.

Out of the blue.

Over time.

Memory by memory.